Helping Children See Jesus

ISBN: 978-1-64104-038-9

THE ETERNAL GOD
Jesus Came into the World
New Testament Volume 1: Life of Christ Part 1

Author: Ruth B. Greiner
Illustrator: Frances H. Hertzler   Front Cover: Linda McInturff
Computer Graphic Artist: Jonthan Ober
Typesetting and Layout: Morgan Melton, Patricia Pope

© 2018 Bible Visuals International
PO Box 153, Akron, PA 17501-0153
Phone: (717) 859-1131
www.biblevisuals.org

All rights reserved. No part of this publication may be reproduced, stored in a retrieval system or transmitted in any form by any means, electronic, mechanical, photocopy, recording or otherwise, without the prior permission of the publisher, except as provided by USA copyright law.

RELATED ITEMS

To access related items (such as activities, memory verse posters and translated texts) please visit our web store at shop.biblevisuals.org and enter 1001 in the search box on the page.

FREE TEXT DOWNLOAD

To access a FREE printable copy of the teaching text (PDF format) in English or other available languages, enter S1001DL in the search box. Add the item to your cart, and use coupon code XTACSV17 at checkout. Once your order is processed you will receive an email with a link to the free download.

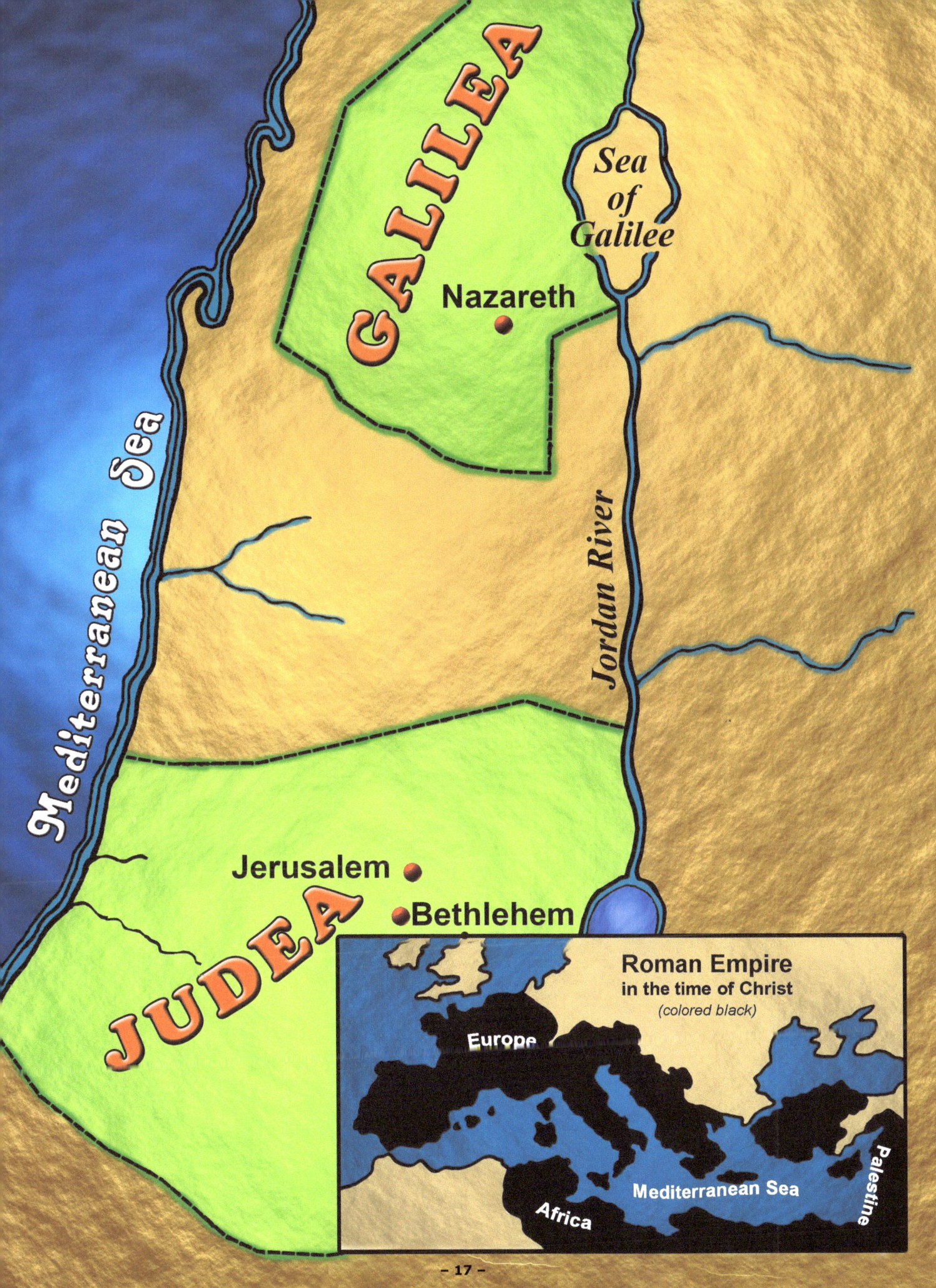

In this was manifested the love of God toward us, because that God sent His only begotten Son into the world, that we might live through Him. 1 John 4:9

Lesson 1
THE PROMISE OF GOD

Scripture to be studied: Luke 1:26-38; Matthew 1:18-25

The *aim* of the lesson: To show that God keeps His promises, even seemingly impossible promises, though He may take long years to fulfill them.

What your students should *know*: God is everywhere, He knows everything and can do anything.

What your students should *feel*: Conscious that God, who knows everything, knows they have sinned.

What your students should *do*: Believe on the Lord Jesus Christ and receive Him as Saviour.

Lesson outline (for the teacher's and students' notebooks):
1. God has no beginning and no end (Psalm 90:2).
2. Prophets recorded the promises of God (Luke 1:70).
3. Mary, chosen to be the mother of Christ (Luke 1:26-38).
4. Christ's birth revealed to Joseph (Matthew 1:18-25).

The verse to be memorized:

In this was manifested [revealed] the love of God toward us, because that God sent His only begotten Son into the world, that we might live through Him. (1 John 4:9)

NOTE TO THE TEACHER

You are going to enjoy teaching the four lessons in this book. Each one has to do with the coming of the Son of God to earth. Because the Word of God is a living Book, the truths in it can–and will–live, first to us who are teachers, and then to those whom we teach.

Try to put yourself in the place of the people in these lessons. If an angel came to you as he did to Mary and to Joseph, you would be amazed surely. Share that amazement with your students. These events really took place. When you tell something thrilling to another, you tell it enthusiastically. Tell these true events from the Word of God with that same kind of enthusiasm.

THE LESSON

1. GOD HAS NO BEGINNING AND NO END
Psalm 90:2

Show Illustration #1

Long, long ago there was no earth. There were no trees, no flowers, no houses, no people. There was no sky or sun or moon. There were no stars or planets. But there was God. God always was. God always will be. As the circle in our illustration has no beginning or no ending, so God has no beginning or ending. He always was. He always will be.

Where is God? He is *everywhere*. (See Psalm 139:1-17.) Only God could be everywhere at once because He *can do anything*–anything that is right. God would not, could not, do wrong.

This wonderful God who is everywhere and can do anything also *knows everything*, even before things happen.

Before the beginning of time, God had a plan–a plan about Heaven, a plan about earth, a plan about people, about His Son and about you! (See Proverbs 8:22-30.)

God planned that the heaven and earth would be beautiful. He planned that the first man and woman He would make and place on earth would be perfect. They would live in the Garden of Eden.

But God knew more. God knew that something terrible would happen–that Adam and Eve, the first man and woman, would disobey Him. Disobeying God is sin. Because of this, God knew that each man and woman, each boy and girl who would live after Adam and Eve would be a sinner.

God was very sad about this. He wanted all the people who would live on the earth to come to live with Him some day in His home, Heaven. Heaven is even more lovely than the earth. But God could never let His home be spoiled by sin or bad things or evil people. (See Revelation 21:27.)

God loved all people. (See John 3:16.) He loved every person who would ever live on the earth. He loved them even though He knew they would be sinners and would lie and cheat and steal and disobey. He loved you before you were born, for He knew about you. He knew where you would be born–and when. He knew where you would live. He knew, too, that you would sin. God knows everything!

When time began, everything happened exactly as God knew it would happen. When He placed the first man and woman, Adam and Eve, on the earth, He made them able to choose between doing right and wrong. God wanted Adam and Eve to love Him and to obey Him.

But Adam and Eve wanted to have their own way. So they disobeyed God. The minute they did that, everything was changed. Instead of being able to enjoy talking with God each day as they had always done, they were ashamed to talk with Him. So they hid from Him. But God had made Adam and Eve so He and they could enjoy each other. He wanted them to be happy on the beautiful earth He had created and, later, in a more beautiful place, His home, Heaven. All of this was changed the moment Adam and Eve sinned.

God knew it was His enemy, Satan, who had caused Adam and Eve to be disobedient. So He promised He would send His Son to earth. He told Satan, His enemy, that His Son would overcome sin and Satan himself! (See Genesis 3:15.) God's wonderful Son would bring everlasting life to all.

2. PROPHETS RECORDED THE PROMISES OF GOD
Luke 1:70

Show Illustration #2

Again and again God repeated His promise that He would send His Son. He told His promise to men called prophets. (See Luke 1:70.) The prophets wrote the promise on scrolls.

One of the great prophets (Isaiah) wrote down this promise of God about His Son who was to come: "And His name shall be called Wonderful, Counsellor, The Mighty God, The Everlasting Father, The Prince of Peace" (Isaiah 9:6).

God also promised, "Behold a virgin shall conceive, and bear a Son and shall call His name Immanuel" (Isaiah 7:14). The prophet wrote this down.

God promised another prophet (Micah) that His Son would be born in the city of Bethlehem. (See Micah 5:2.)

The prophets wrote down these and many other promises of God. The people heard and read those promises. They waited and waited. They hoped. When would the Son of God be born? When would the promises come true? Hundreds and hundreds of years passed after God made His first promise. Some believed His promise would come true. Others did not believe.

3. MARY, CHOSEN TO BE THE MOTHER OF CHRIST
Luke 1:26-38

Many Jewish women waited and wondered, each wishing she might be the mother of the wonderful Child whom God had promised.

Mary was a young Jewish woman who loved God very much. (See Luke 1:26-38.) She, too, was waiting for the promised One who would some day be King. When would He come?

Show Illustration #3

While we do not know exactly all that happened, apparently one day Mary's little room in Nazareth was suddenly filled with a great brightness. Mary was afraid, for standing there was a shining angel! The angel Gabriel, who was sent from God, spoke: "Do not be afraid, Mary. God is pleased with you. Listen! You are going to have a Son. You will call His name Jesus. He will be great and shall be called the Son of the Most High God."

"But–but I am not married. How can this be?" Mary asked her heavenly visitor.

"Through the power of God it shall be. There is not one thing God cannot do," the angel answered.

Mary could not understand all that this wonderful promise would mean or how it would happen. But she believed.

"I am the Lord's servant," Mary answered. "Let it happen as you have said."

When Gabriel left, Mary wondered, *Am I really the one chosen to be the mother of the Son of God–the Child promised long ago?* Yes, it was true.

But who would be the Father of the Child? His Father would be God. Nothing so wonderful had ever happened since the earth was made. The time had come for God to make sure His promise.

4. CHRIST'S BIRTH REVEALED TO JOSEPH
Matthew 1:18-25

Mary had to tell her great secret to someone. She chose to tell Joseph, a good man whom she loved and had promised to marry. When he heard the strange news, he could not understand how such a thing could be. (See Matthew 1:18-25.) He thought he should not marry this young woman, even though he loved her.

Show Illustration #4

One night an angel of the Lord stood before him. "Joseph," the angel said, "do not be afraid to take Mary to be your wife. Her child will be the Son of God. You will call His name JESUS: for He will save His people from their sins."

When Joseph awoke, the angel had disappeared. But Joseph remembered the message of the angel of God. This Child would be the Son of God. But he, Joseph, would have the honor of caring for God's Son.

"He will save His people from their sins," the angel had said. Joseph thought of those words. What did they mean? How would this Baby, the Son of God, save His people from their sins?

Joseph may not have understood all that the angel had said. Perhaps he did not realize that the One who was to be born would die for the sins of the world. He may not have understood. But Joseph believed God. And Mary believed God.

Do you believe God? Do you believe He sent His Son exactly as He promised, to save people from their sins? Do you believe in His Son, the wonderful Lord Jesus Christ? Have you received Him as your Saviour? If you have never done so, and if you truly believe He is the Son of God, ask Him to forgive your sin and invite Him to live in your heart and life. Do it this very minute.

NOTE TO THE TEACHER

Pray that some who hear this lesson will respond to the invitation to believe on the Lord Jesus Christ and receive Him as Saviour. If at all possible, talk with any who make this decision. There are suggestions on the inside back cover to be used with those who want to receive the Lord Jesus as Saviour.

All through the lesson keep before the students that God is everywhere; He knows all things; and He can do anything. The angel of the Lord put it this way: "For with God nothing shall be impossible" (Luke 1:37).

As you teach this lesson, you are serving the God of the impossible. May He make the truths of His Word clear to you–and to those you teach.

Lesson 2
THE BIRTH OF THE LORD JESUS

Scripture to be studied: Luke 2:1-7

The aim of the lesson: To show that the Lord Jesus Christ, who was born of the Virgin Mary, is God the Son.

What your students should *know*: That Jesus Christ is the Son of God.

What your students should *feel*: A desire to have assurance of salvation.

What your students should *do*: Receive the Lord Jesus as their Saviour from sin.

Lesson outline (for the teacher's and students' notebooks):
1. The new decree (Luke 2:1-2).
2. The journey to Bethlehem (Luke 2:3-5).
3. The crowded inn (Luke 2:6-7).
4. The birth of Christ (Luke 2:6-7).

The verse to be memorized:

In this was manifested [revealed] the love of God toward us, because that God sent His only begotten Son into the world, that we might live through Him. (1 John 4:9)

THE LESSON

Almost always in every village and every city and every country, there is one who is in charge. He may be a chief, a king, a governor, or a president. It is so today. It was so in the long ago. The Roman Empire was large and great in the long ago. The ruler of the empire was called an emperor.

> **NOTE TO THE TEACHER**
>
> Did you enjoy teaching the first lesson, *The Promise of God*? It is glorious to belong to the God of the impossible!
>
> Before reading the next lesson as it is written here, read the account in the Bible, Luke 2:1-7. Do you suppose that when Emperor Caesar Augustus signed his decree, God in Heaven laughed? Read Psalm 2:1-4. The Emperor made it necessary for Mary and Joseph to go to Bethlehem. But 700 years before that, the prophet Micah had said that the Son of God would be born in Bethlehem (Micah 5:2)! God causes the wrath of man to praise Him. (See Psalm 76:10.)

1. THE NEW DECREE
Luke 2:1-2

Show Illustration #5

Emperor Caesar Augustus sat at a table in his royal palace. Sternly he studied the new law he had just signed. He, the powerful ruler of all the Roman Empire, had made this law and no one could change it!

He doubtless wondered what the people would say about the new command. It would mean great hardship for many. But this did not matter to him, the great Caesar Augustus!

Calling his soldiers together, he announced, "This is my new law! Make it known in every country of my empire. Listen carefully! Every man and woman must go to the city or town from which his family came. There he must register his name for me, Emperor Augustus."

To himself he thought, *From the names on this list I shall be able to collect lots of money for the Roman Government. Also, I can order many men, whose names I shall get when they register, to enlist in my army to make it mighty. Everyone will know that I, the great Emperor Caesar Augustus, am strong and powerful.*

The emperor spoke again: "See to it that every man and woman hears the order–and that everyone obeys!"

2. THE JOURNEY TO BETHLEHEM
Luke 2:3-5

The soldiers went to every part of the empire to spread the word. Soon men and women began to move in obedience to the emperor's command. In a small country (Galilee) within the Roman Empire, a young couple, Joseph and Mary, heard the new law. They had come from the town of Bethlehem where King David had been born more than a thousand years before. Because of that, Bethlehem had become known as the City of David. To obey the command of the emperor, Mary and Joseph would have to make the long journey from their home in Nazareth (of Galilee) to Bethlehem (in Judea)–about 80 miles!

Must they go? Yes! The great Emperor Augustus had made the command. Everyone had to obey. Mary and Joseph prepared for the journey. They packed the food and clothing they would need and started on their way.

Show Illustration #6

Mary and Joseph traveled on dangerous roads, across many hills. As they made their journey, God watched over them and protected them each long day. God was with them as they rested in the stillness of the night.

One thing made both Mary and Joseph happy as they went. It was the wonderful secret God had shared with them through the angel. Mary was to have a Baby who would be different from every other child–He would be the Saviour of the world. God would be His Father. Joseph, too, had been honored, for he would have the special privilege of caring for the Baby and for Mary, the Child's mother. It was all in the plan of God.

But Mary was very tired. Joseph was also weary. When would they reach Bethlehem? It seemed like an endless journey.

At last Joseph exclaimed, "There it is! There is the town of Bethlehem! Soon you'll be able to rest. I'll find a place where we can stay for the night– a quiet place where you can sleep."

3. THE CROWDED INN
Luke 2:6-7

But Bethlehem was crowded. There were many people who had come to register their names.

Show Illustration #7

We shall surely find a place in the inn, Joseph thought. Mary was quiet as Joseph asked for a room.

"No room! No room!" the innkeeper told him.

– 21 –

"But there must be one room," Joseph said. "We've come all the way from Nazareth. Look at my wife. She is tired. She needs a place to sleep. Please! There must be room for us."

"I'm sorry. Every room in my inn is occupied. I tell you again! There is no room!"

"But what will we do?" Joseph asked. "Is there no way you can help us?"

"Yes, there is a place. But it's only a stable. You wouldn't want to stay there. It's all right for sheep and donkeys. But you would not want to stay there."

"We'll take it," Joseph said quickly.

So Mary and Joseph were led to a small stable. Darkness had already fallen in Bethlehem and the homes were quiet. Mothers and fathers, boys and girls, were asleep. But Mary and Joseph could not sleep.

God was looking down upon the earth He had made: the trees and flowers and grass continued to grow exactly as He had planned. The stars shone in the night sky right where He had placed them. The sun, moon, the oceans, lakes, rivers, the fish, birds and animals all acted according to the commands of God. All things obeyed the One who had made them.

4. THE BIRTH OF CHRIST
Luke 2:6-7

This same God had also planned that this would be the night when the Saviour, His own dear Son, would come in person to live on earth–to live as a baby, a boy, a man. This One, the Eternal Son, had created the earth with God. (See John 1:3; Ephesians 3:9.) Now God the Father was sending His Son to be born on the earth which He had created. And Bethlehem was the town in which God had promised His Son would be born.

Show Illustration #8

God the Son was born not in a palace or a glorious mansion but in a stable–and in Bethlehem, just as the prophet had promised. (See Micah 5:2.)

The marvelous moment was both solemn and sacred as Mary saw the perfect Child for the very first time. Gently she held Him close in her arms. How she loved Him! Tenderly she touched His soft hands and face. Ever so gently Mary laid her dear Treasure in a manger.

Joseph looked down in wonder at the Son of God, the Altogether Lovely One. Never had One like this been born.

The promise of God had come true! (See Isaiah 7:14; 9:6; 11:1-5.) God knew! Mary knew! Joseph knew! God the Son was living on earth as a Baby. The whole world should know of the wonderful miracle–a miracle which only God could do.

In the stable all was well. God's plan had marvelously come to pass.

But what a change in Heaven! God the Father had sent His Son to live on earth among sinners. Why did He let Him go? Was it because He cared about you and me? Yes! God loved us so much that He sent His only Son to earth to be our Saviour from sin. He was the gift of God for you–for all of you!

Today, over 2,000 years later, God is waiting for you to receive His love gift. By believing that the Lord Jesus is the Son of God, by inviting Him to live in your heart, your sins will be forgiven and you will receive the gift of God–eternal life. The Lord Jesus wants to be your Saviour.

> **NOTE TO THE TEACHER**
>
> As you prepare this lesson and as you teach it, why not to make this your prayer: "Dear Father in Heaven, help me to make clear the great truth of this lesson. Help me to speak with such conviction, and let the verses from the Bible be so clear, that each one I teach will realize that Jesus Christ is truly the Son of God. Help me to show my students how they can have the assurance of eternal life. May each one have the joy of sins forgiven."
>
> Remember, the Lord Jesus is praying for you!

Lesson 3
VISITORS TO THE KING

Scripture to be studied: Luke 2:8-20; Matthew 2:1-18.

The *aim* of the lesson: To show that the Son of God is worthy of our best.

What your students should *know*: That the Lord Jesus is the Saviour of the world.

What your students should *feel*: Willing to receive Christ and tell others of Him.

What your students should *do*:
  Unsaved: Believe in the Lord Jesus Christ.
  Saved: Tell their friends of Christ, the Saviour.

Lesson outline (for the teacher's and students' notebooks):
1. Angels announce Christ's birth (Luke 2:8-15).
2. Shepherds worship Christ (Luke 2:16-20).
3. Wise men follow the star (Matthew 2:1-10).
4. Wise men worship Christ (Matthew 2:11-12).

The verse to be memorized:

In this was manifested [revealed] the love of God toward us, because that God sent His only begotten Son into the world, that we might live through Him. (1 John 4:9)

> **NOTE TO THE TEACHER**
>
> Before reading the lesson as it is written here, please read Luke 2:8-20 and Matthew 2:1-18. Study these verses carefully, prayerfully. Though we ourselves have read these sections many times, as we prepared this lesson we found brand new truths. This is the wonderful thing about the Bible. It always has something fresh to say to us.
>
> What should be your purpose for teaching this lesson? Study the Scriptures carefully so you can determine one special aim you should have when you teach this material.

THE LESSON

On a quiet hillside near Bethlehem (in Judea), shepherds guarded their flocks. They watched carefully so that no wild animal would attack their sleeping sheep. Stars twinkled brightly against the darkness of the night sky. All was still except for the hushed voices of the shepherds as they talked and warmed themselves beside the fire.

The shepherds doubtless felt sad because things were not right in the land of Palestine. Their ruler did not love God. Many of the people had forgotten the promise that God had given again and again through His prophets–the promise about the Saviour who was to come. Even the shepherds wondered when the promised One would come–the One who would be both Saviour and King. They had waited long. Their fathers and grandfathers had waited, too. The shepherds believed God. But how much longer would they have to wait?

1. ANGELS ANNOUNCE CHRIST'S BIRTH
Luke 2:8-15

Show Illustration #9

Suddenly the sky grew bright. The darkness disappeared. The shepherds blinked their eyes. For an angel, bright and shining, appeared before them. The shepherds were frightened. They hid their eyes from the light.

"Don't be afraid!" the angel commanded. "I bring you the most joyful news ever told. It is for everyone. This night, your Saviour is born in Bethlehem, the city of David. Go and see! You will find Him wrapped in soft clothing, lying in a manger."

Then, before the shepherds could move or speak, many, many angels appeared. Joyfully the angels praised God and said, "Glory to God in the highest Heaven! And peace on earth to men who are pleasing Him."

When their glorious message ended, the angels disappeared.

The shepherds stared at the empty sky. Then they looked at one another uncertainly. Could it be that the promise of God made long ago had come true? Was it true that a baby born this very night in Bethlehem was the Saviour of the world–their Saviour?

"Come!" they exclaimed. "Let us go at once to Bethlehem and see this miracle about which the angels spoke." The shepherds left sheep on the hillside and started for Bethlehem. They must see this wonderful Child–the Saviour!

2. SHEPHERDS WORSHIP CHRIST
Luke 2:16-20

At last they found the place where Jesus had been born. It was not a palace, not a mansion, not even a humble home, but a stable. The shepherds knew all about stables and mangers where animals slept and ate. But why had the Saviour been born in a stable? Was it because God wanted poor people to know that He loved them?

Show Illustration #10

Joseph welcomed the shepherds at the doorway and led them inside. The visitors tiptoed to the manger. Then they saw Him of whom the angels had spoken–the promised One from God. He was sinless. But He had come to this earth for an important reason–to take upon Himself the sin of the world. The shepherds would have wept if they had known that this precious One would some day suffer and die for their sins. But the shepherds were not sad now. They rejoiced that the Saviour had come from God. They were seeing Him with their very own eyes.

Leaving the quiet place where the Son of God lay, they told the good news to everyone they met: "The Saviour of the world has been born. He has come to earth. We saw Him in a stable in Bethlehem. He is the One for Whom we have been waiting."

Joyfully the shepherds returned to their sheep. But they continued to praise God and give thanks for all the things they had heard and seen.

3. WISE MEN FOLLOW THE STAR
Matthew 2:1-10

Show Illustration #11

But all was not well in the land. One day word reached Herod, the ruler of the land of Palestine, that some strangers from a far-away eastern land had come to Jerusalem. They were seeking a new King who had been born. They said they had been studying the stars and suddenly they had seen one which had never before been seen. The new star meant to them that a Baby had been born–a Baby who was to be the King of the Jews.

How dare they look for a new King! thought Herod. *I am the king of all this land. No one shall take my place.*

He called together the chief priests and teachers. "Tell me," he ordered, "where is the Christ-child to be born?"

"We have read in the prophecies of Micah, O King, that the One who is to be Ruler of the Jews will be born in Bethlehem."

Herod was afraid. He, the great Herod, was king. He wanted always to be king–the only king!

Herod dismissed the teachers and the chief priests. Then he called for a secret meeting with the wise strangers. He asked them when they had seen the star. He pretended to be interested in the new-born King. "Go to Bethlehem," he told the wise men. "Look carefully for the Child. When you find Him let me know so that I, too, may go and worship Him."

The wise men hurried toward Bethlehem. And, as they left Jerusalem, they saw the star–the special star they had first seen in the East. How glad they were! They knew that they would soon see the King. The star moved before them and stopped over a house. No longer was the Baby lying in a manger. He, with Mary and Joseph, had moved to one of the small homes along the narrow streets of Bethlehem. The wise men had traveled far. But at last the wonderful moment had arrived. They were about to see the One whose star they had followed.

4. WISE MEN WORSHIP CHRIST
Matthew 2:11-12

Show Illustration #12

As they entered the house, the wise men carried gifts they had brought from their land–gifts of gold, incense and myrrh. When they saw the young child with Mary, His mother, they bowed low with great awe and worshiped the Son of God. The men from the East did not think of their wealth, or their power, or their great wisdom. They thought only of the One they had come to see. Did they know how rich, how great and how wise He really was? Compared to His greatness, their gifts seemed small. But they gave them to the One who was the gift of God to men on earth–the greatest Gift ever given.

That night God warned the wise men in a dream that they should not go back to King Herod in Jerusalem. So, in obedience to God, they returned to their land another way.

We do not know exactly what the wise men thought when they brought their expensive gifts to the Son of God. Sometimes gifts have particular meanings. And it may be that the wise man who gave gold–a gift often given to kings–was thinking, *Jesus is truly the King.*

Incense was used by priests in their worship of God. The wise man who gave incense may have thought, *The Lord Jesus is a Priest, the One who will pray for us.*

The one who gave myrrh–something that was used on the bodies of those who had died–may have thought, *This is the Promised One from God–the One who will die for my sins.* (Read Psalm 22 and Isaiah 53:2-9.)

Today, hundreds of years later, the Lord Jesus is praying for you. He is praying that you will become a member of the family of God. You may become part of the family of God by believing that the Son of God is the One who died for the sin of the world, and by inviting Him to be your Saviour. By receiving Him you give Him the most important gift of all–yourself.

We have no way of knowing *exactly* what the shepherds thought when they looked into the face of the Son of God. They were too poor to bring gifts. But, oh, how they loved Him! And, loving Him, they went everywhere telling others about Him. Will you tell someone about the Saviour today–this week?

> **NOTE TO THE TEACHER**
> If those you are teaching are already believers in the Lord Jesus Christ, you could add this thought to the lesson: The Lord Jesus will one day rule the world as King. Right now, however, He is waiting for you to invite Him to control your life. He will be the King of your life only if you ask Him to do so. Will you do so right now?

Lesson 4
JESUS IS ETERNAL

> **NOTE TO THE TEACHER**
>
> There are six important facts to remember in teaching this lesson:
>
> 1. The Lord Jesus is the Son of God.
> 2. The Lord Jesus, the Creator, can do all things.
> 3. The Lord Jesus knows all things.
> 4. The Lord Jesus is perfect.
> 5. The Lord Jesus died for the sin of the world.
> 6. The Lord Jesus is God the Son.
>
> Make it clear to your students that Christ existed before He was born in Bethlehem. He is eternal. (See Isaiah 9:6; Micah 5:2; compare John 8:58.) While the Lord Jesus was on earth, He explained that He is one with God the Father. (See John 5:18; 10:30.) When He spoke of Himself as "the Son of God" (John 10:36), it was perfectly understood that He identified Himself as God, equal with the Father. Those who wrote the New Testament also spoke of His equality with God. (See, for example, John 1:1; 20:28; Romans 9:5; Philippians 2:6; Titus 2:13.)
>
> Christ Himself made it plain that He is able to do certain things which only God can do: He has power to forgive sins (Mark 2:1-12); All judgment was given into His hands (John 5:27); He promised to send the Holy Spirit (John 15:26); He announced that He would raise the dead (John 5:25).
>
> It is also clear that certain works, which God alone can do, were performed by Christ the Lord: He created all things (John 1:3; Colossians 1:16); He upholds all things (Colossians 1:17; Hebrews 1:3); He is the Judge of all (Acts 17:31).
>
> The Lord Jesus has characteristics which only God has: He spoke of His being all-powerful (Matthew 28:18; Revelation 1:8); He has all-knowledge (Mark 2:8; John 1:48); He is everywhere-present (Matthew 18:20; 28:20); He is worshiped by men and angels (Matthew 14:33; Philippians 2:10; Hebrews 1:6); God the Son is mentioned along with God the Father and God the Holy Spirit–all being equal (Matthew 28:19; 2 Corinthians 13:14).
>
> That Christ is one with God is proved also by His names: God (Hebrews 1:8); Lord (Matthew 22:43-45); King of kings and Lord of lords (Revelation 19:16).
>
> The Lord Jesus is fully God but He is also fully Man. He is like all humanity, with one important exception: He is without sin.
>
> Although Christ was always with God the Father, He came to earth in flesh. He was born of a virgin (Isaiah 7:14; Matthew 1:23); miraculously Fathered by the Holy Spirit of God (Luke 1:35).
>
> Christ the Lord came to earth to:
> - reveal God to people (John 1:18)
> - be an example (1 Peter 2:21)
> - provide a sacrifice for sin (Hebrews 10:1-10)
> - destroy the works of the devil (1 John 3:8)
> - enable Him to be a merciful and faithful High Priest (Hebrews 5:1-2)
> - fulfill the promise of a Son to sit upon the throne of David forever (Luke 1:31-33)
>
> Only a person can die. So the Lord Jesus had to come in a body of flesh in order to be able to die. Because He lived on earth as a Man, He can understand and sympathize as our Priest.
>
> > **IMPORTANT TO REMEMBER:**
> > Christ is fully God and perfect Man. (See Hebrews 4:15; 2 Corinthians 5:21.)
> > His two natures–God and Man–are united in one person: Jesus Christ the Lord.

Scripture to be studied: John 1:1-14; Colossians 1:15-19; Hebrews 1:1-3

The *aim* of the lesson: To show that the Son of God is both perfect God and perfect Man.

What your students should *know*: What great love God had in sending His only Son to earth to live and to die.

What your students should *feel*: Because of sins, unworthy of His great love.

What your students should *do*: Believe that Jesus Christ is the Son of God and receive Him as Saviour.

Lesson outline (for the teacher's and students' notebooks):
1. Jesus Christ is the Creator (John 1:3; Colossians 1:16).
2. Jesus Christ is perfect (John 8:29; 2 Corinthians 5:21).
3. Jesus Christ is Man–God with us (Matthew 1:23).
4. Jesus Christ is the Saviour (John 3:16-19).

Have your students memorized 1 John 4:9?

In this was manifested [revealed] the love of God toward us, because God sent His only begotten Son into the world, that we might live through Him. (1 John 4:9)

Do they understand the verse? These lessons should have made the meaning perfectly clear.

THE LESSON

Many, many babies have been born since the day God made the first man and woman, Adam and Eve. But of all the babies ever born, the most important was the Lord Jesus Christ. He was born long ago in the town of Bethlehem. He was so special that angels came from Heaven to tell of His birth. They announced the wonderful news to shepherds on a quiet hillside. This baby was so important and wonderful that a special star appeared in the sky to lead far-away wise men to worship Him.

Why is the Lord Jesus so important? Why did the prophets in the Old Testament talk about His coming hundreds of years before He was born? Why did angels adore Him? Why did shepherds worship Him? Why did the wise men bring rich gifts to Him?

The Lord Jesus is important because He is the Son of God. He had lived with His Father, God, in Heaven. He had always lived–before there was a town called Bethlehem, before a star ever shone in the sky, before there was a moon or sun, before the earth was made. (See John 17:5.) The Son of God is eternal. "Eternal" means *no beginning and no ending*. The Lord Jesus had no beginning and He will have no end. Jesus has always been and He always will be.

1. JESUS CHRIST IS THE CREATOR
John 1:3; Colossians 1:16

Show Illustration #13

Because Jesus is the Son of God, He can do anything. He can make anything. Long before He was born in Bethlehem, He and His Father made the sun and placed it in the sky. "All things were made by Him," the Word of God tells us. (Read John 1:3.) The earth, the trees, the grass, the birds, the fish, the animals, man and woman–all were made by Him. The Lord Jesus Christ is the Creator–the Maker of all things. (See Colossians 1:16; Hebrews 1:10.) When He left Heaven and came to earth, He was indeed a special Baby!

Not only can the Lord Jesus do all things, but He knows all things. (See John 16:30.) He knows what you think. He knows what you do. (See Matthew 9:4.) He knows all about you.

2. JESUS CHRIST IS PERFECT
John 8:29; 2 Corinthians 5:21

The eternal Son of God, who can do all things and knows all things, is perfect! He has never sinned. (See John 8:29.) He will never do one thing that is wrong. He will never think a wrong thought, speak an evil word, or do a wrong deed. (See 2 Corinthians 5:21.)

This wonderful Lord Jesus could have stayed in Heaven with His Father. But if He had, no man or woman, boy or girl could ever have gone to live with Him in Heaven.

Show Illustration #14

Do you know why none of us could have gone to Heaven? It is because God is perfectly good and He cannot allow sin in His Heaven. Everything in Heaven is perfect and beautiful. It is a place of light. But all people everywhere have hearts full of sin and darkness. They love the darkness more than the light for their deeds are evil. (See John 3:19.) The sin of their hearts has, like a great stone wall, kept them from God and His marvelous light.

Of all the people born since Adam and Eve, no one has been without sin, except the Lord Jesus only. Jesus is the only Man who ever lived who is worthy to live in Heaven. And He is the only One who can take away our sin. That is why He came down to earth.

The Lord Jesus is different from all other people in that He chose to obey God. The first two on earth, Adam and Eve, chose to disobey God. Disobeying God is sin. God wants us to choose to obey Him. We cannot do this by ourselves. We, like Adam and Eve, are sinners. We are separated from God because of our sin.

3. JESUS CHRIST IS MAN– GOD WITH US
Matthew 1:23

But God loved Adam and Eve, and God loves you and me. So He promised to send One who would save them–and us–from sin. (See Genesis 3:15.) This One would not be an angel, but a Man–a Man who, though born to a human mother, would be different from every other child who would ever be born.

All through the years God repeated over and over again the promise of the One to come. Some of the promises said that God Himself would come to earth. (See Isaiah 7:14. His very name *Immanuel,* means *God with us* as we are told in Matthew 1:23. See also Isaiah 25:9; Isaiah 40:10.) But how could the One to come be both God and Man? Could God be born on earth as other babies are?

Long before the worlds were formed, it had been decided that the One to come to earth would be God the Son. He would come as a Baby. He would grow as a Child and as a Man. But there would be a difference. He would be perfect. Because He would be perfect He could take the punishment for the sins of others, the sins of the entire world!

Show Illustration #15

What did it really mean for the Son of God to come to earth and become Man? It meant leaving His wonderful home in beautiful Heaven. Instead of living with His Father, He came to live among sinners. (See Philippians 2:5-8.) He might have come to earth as an angel, but He came as a helpless Baby. He might have come to live in a royal palace. But He came into the home of a carpenter. Oh, how much He gave up for us! God the Son willingly came to live and die for the sins of the whole world. He came for you and for me. There is no greater love than that of Jesus Christ for us. When God the Son became Man, He did not stop being God. He was God living in a human body. Never, never forget it: the Lord Jesus Christ is God with us.

4. JESUS CHRIST IS THE SAVIOUR
John 3:16-19

Show Illustration #16

As had been planned before the earth was formed, God the Son one day died on a cross. He, the sinless One, took the punishment for the sins of the whole world! He, knowing all people everywhere, knew they chose darkness rather than His light. He knew that the punishment for choosing sin and darkness was to be forever separated from God. And He does not want anyone anywhere to be separated from God. So He–the perfect One–died on the cross for all. He died for you, for me.

Now, no matter how poor or small we may be, we can come to the Lord Jesus. He will receive us and forgive our sin. He is waiting this moment to cleanse your sinful heart. He will do this when you believe He is the Son of God, and when you believe He paid the penalty for your sin when He died on the cross. Do you believe this? Have you asked Him to forgive your sin? Have you received Him as your Saviour?

TEACHER, THIS COULD BE YOUR PRAYER . . .

Dear Heavenly Father, help me to show in Your own way that the Lord Jesus Christ is perfect God and perfect Man. Through this lesson may each student know of Your great love in sending Your Son as a sacrifice for sin. May each one of us feel how unworthy we are of Your love and Your gift of the Lord Jesus. I pray that each one in my group will come to know Christ as personal Saviour from sin. Make me the kind of teacher I ought to be. Amen.